Drug Name

_____

Drug Uses

Side Effects

Notes

Drug Name

_____

Drug Uses

Side Effects

Notes

Drug Name

Drug Uses

Side Effects

Notes

Drug Name

Drug Uses

Side Effects

Notes

Drug Name

_____

Drug Uses

Side Effects

Notes

Drug Name

Drug Uses

Side Effects

Notes

Drug Name

Drug Uses

Side Effects

Notes

Drug Name

_____

Drug Uses

Side Effects

Notes

Drug Name

Drug Uses

Side Effects

Notes

Drug Name

Drug Uses

Side Effects

Notes

Drug Name

_____

Drug Uses

Side Effects

Notes

Drug Name

Drug Uses

Side Effects

Notes

Drug Name

Drug Uses

Side Effects

Notes

Drug Name

Drug Uses

Side Effects

Notes

Drug Name

Drug Uses

Side Effects

Notes

Drug Name

Drug Uses

Side Effects

Notes

Drug Name

Drug Uses

Side Effects

Notes

Drug Name

Drug Uses

Side Effects

Notes

Drug Name

Drug Uses

Side Effects

Notes

Drug Name

_____

Drug Uses

Side Effects

Notes

Drug Name

Drug Uses

Side Effects

Notes

Drug Name

Drug Uses

Side Effects

Notes

Drug Name

Drug Uses

Side Effects

Notes

Drug Name

Drug Uses

Side Effects

Notes

Drug Name

Drug Uses

Side Effects

Notes

Drug Name

Drug Uses

Side Effects

Notes

Drug Name

Drug Uses

Side Effects

Notes

Drug Name

Drug Uses

Side Effects

Notes

Drug Name

Drug Uses

Side Effects

Notes

Drug Name

Drug Uses

Side Effects

Notes

Drug Name

Drug Uses

Side Effects

Notes

Drug Name

Drug Uses

Side Effects

Notes

Drug Name

_____

Drug Uses

Side Effects

Notes

Drug Name

Drug Uses

Side Effects

Notes

Drug Name

Drug Uses

Side Effects

Notes

Drug Name

Drug Uses

Side Effects

Notes

Drug Name

Drug Uses

Side Effects

Notes

Drug Name

Drug Uses

Side Effects

Notes

Drug Name

Drug Uses

Side Effects

Notes

Drug Name

Drug Uses

Side Effects

Notes

Drug Name

Drug Uses

Side Effects

Notes

Drug Name

_____

Drug Uses

Side Effects

Notes

Drug Name

Drug Uses

Side Effects

Notes

Drug Name

Drug Uses

Side Effects

Notes

Drug Name

Drug Uses

Side Effects

Notes

Drug Name

Drug Uses

Side Effects

Notes

Drug Name

Drug Uses

Side Effects

Notes

Drug Name

Drug Uses

Side Effects

Notes

Drug Name

Drug Uses

Side Effects

Notes

Drug Name

Drug Uses

Side Effects

Notes

Drug Name

Drug Uses

Side Effects

Notes

Drug Name

Drug Uses

Side Effects

Notes

Drug Name

Drug Uses

Side Effects

Notes

Drug Name

Drug Uses

Side Effects

Notes

Drug Name

_____

Drug Uses

Side Effects

Notes

Drug Name

_____

Drug Uses

Side Effects

Notes

Drug Name

Drug Uses

Side Effects

Notes

Drug Name

Drug Uses

Side Effects

Notes

Drug Name

Drug Uses

Side Effects

Notes

Drug Name

Drug Uses

Side Effects

Notes

Drug Name

Drug Uses

Side Effects

Notes

Drug Name

Drug Uses

Side Effects

Notes

Drug Name

Drug Uses

Side Effects

Notes

Drug Name

Drug Uses

Side Effects

Notes

Drug Name

_____

Drug Uses

Side Effects

Notes

Drug Name

Drug Uses

Side Effects

Notes

Drug Name

Drug Uses

Side Effects

Notes

Drug Name

Drug Uses

Side Effects

Notes

Drug Name

Drug Uses

Side Effects

Notes

Drug Name

Drug Uses

Side Effects

Notes

Drug Name

Drug Uses

Side Effects

Notes

Drug Name

Drug Uses

Side Effects

Notes

Drug Name

_____

Drug Uses

Side Effects

Notes

Drug Name

Drug Uses

Side Effects

Notes

Drug Name

Drug Uses

Side Effects

Notes

Drug Name

Drug Uses

Side Effects

Notes

Drug Name

_____

Drug Uses

Side Effects

Notes

Drug Name

_____

Drug Uses

Side Effects

Notes

Drug Name

_____

Drug Uses

Side Effects

Notes

Drug Name

Drug Uses

Side Effects

Notes

Drug Name

Drug Uses

Side Effects

Notes

Drug Name

Drug Uses

Side Effects

Notes

Drug Name

_____

Drug Uses

Side Effects

Notes

Drug Name

Drug Uses

Side Effects

Notes

Drug Name

_____

Drug Uses

Side Effects

Notes

Drug Name

_____

Drug Uses

Side Effects

Notes

Drug Name

Drug Uses

Side Effects

Notes

Drug Name

Drug Uses

Side Effects

Notes

Drug Name

Drug Uses

Side Effects

Notes

Drug Name

Drug Uses

Side Effects

Notes

Drug Name

Drug Uses

Side Effects

Notes

Drug Name

Drug Uses

Side Effects

Notes

Drug Name

Drug Uses

Side Effects

Notes

Drug Name

Drug Uses

Side Effects

Notes

Drug Name

Drug Uses

Side Effects

Notes

Drug Name

Drug Uses

Side Effects

Notes

Drug Name

Drug Uses

Side Effects

Notes

Drug Name

_____

Drug Uses

Side Effects

Notes

Drug Name

_____

Drug Uses

Side Effects

Notes

Drug Name

Drug Uses

Side Effects

Notes

Drug Name

Drug Uses

Side Effects

Notes

Drug Name

Drug Uses

Side Effects

Notes

Drug Name

Drug Uses

Side Effects

Notes

Drug Name

Drug Uses

Side Effects

Notes

Drug Name

_____

Drug Uses

Side Effects

Notes

Drug Name

Drug Uses

Side Effects

Notes

Drug Name

Drug Uses

Side Effects

Notes

Drug Name

Drug Uses

Side Effects

Notes

Drug Name

Drug Uses

Side Effects

Notes

Drug Name

Drug Uses

Side Effects

Notes

Drug Name

Drug Uses

Side Effects

Notes

Drug Name

Drug Uses

Side Effects

Notes

Drug Name

Drug Uses

Side Effects

Notes

Drug Name

Drug Uses

Side Effects

Notes

Drug Name

_____

Drug Uses

Side Effects

Notes

Drug Name

Drug Uses

Side Effects

Notes

Drug Name

Drug Uses

Side Effects

Notes

Drug Name

Drug Uses

Side Effects

Notes

Drug Name

Drug Uses

Side Effects

Notes

Drug Name

Drug Uses

Side Effects

Notes

Drug Name

Drug Uses

Side Effects

Notes

Drug Name

Drug Uses

Side Effects

Notes

Drug Name

Drug Uses

Side Effects

Notes

Drug Name

_____

Drug Uses

Side Effects

Notes

Drug Name

Drug Uses

Side Effects

Notes

Drug Name

Drug Uses

Side Effects

Notes

Drug Name

Drug Uses

Side Effects

Notes

Drug Name

Drug Uses

Side Effects

Notes

Drug Name

Drug Uses

Side Effects

Notes

Drug Name

Drug Uses

Side Effects

Notes

Drug Name

_____

Drug Uses

Side Effects

Notes

Drug Name

Drug Uses

Side Effects

Notes

Drug Name

_____

Drug Uses

Side Effects

Notes

Drug Name

Drug Uses

Side Effects

Notes

Drug Name

Drug Uses

Side Effects

Notes

Drug Name

Drug Uses

Side Effects

Notes

Drug Name

Drug Uses

Side Effects

Notes

Drug Name

_____

Drug Uses

Side Effects

Notes

Drug Name

Drug Uses

Side Effects

Notes

Drug Name

Drug Uses

Side Effects

Notes

Drug Name

Drug Uses

Side Effects

Notes

Drug Name

Drug Uses

Side Effects

Notes

Drug Name

Drug Uses

Side Effects

Notes

Drug Name

Drug Uses

Side Effects

Notes

Drug Name

Drug Uses

Side Effects

Notes

Drug Name

_____

Drug Uses

Side Effects

Notes

Drug Name

Drug Uses

Side Effects

Notes

Drug Name

Drug Uses

Side Effects

Notes

Drug Name

Drug Uses

Side Effects

Notes

Drug Name

Drug Uses

Side Effects

Notes

Drug Name

Drug Uses

Side Effects

Notes

Drug Name

Drug Uses

Side Effects

Notes

Drug Name

_____

Drug Uses

Side Effects

Notes

Drug Name

Drug Uses

Side Effects

Notes

Drug Name

Drug Uses

Side Effects

Notes

Drug Name

Drug Uses

Side Effects

Notes

Drug Name

Drug Uses

Side Effects

Notes

Drug Name

Drug Uses

Side Effects

Notes

Drug Name

Drug Uses

Side Effects

Notes

Drug Name

Drug Uses

Side Effects

Notes

Drug Name

Drug Uses

Side Effects

Notes

Drug Name

Drug Uses

Side Effects

Notes

Drug Name

Drug Uses

Side Effects

Notes

Drug Name

Drug Uses

Side Effects

Notes

Drug Name

Drug Uses

Side Effects

Notes

Drug Name

Drug Uses

Side Effects

Notes

Drug Name

Drug Uses

Side Effects

Notes

Drug Name

Drug Uses

Side Effects

Notes

Drug Name

Drug Uses

Side Effects

Notes

Drug Name

Drug Uses

Side Effects

Notes

Drug Name

Drug Uses

Side Effects

Notes

Drug Name

Drug Uses

Side Effects

Notes

Drug Name

Drug Uses

Side Effects

Notes

Drug Name

_____

Drug Uses

Side Effects

Notes

Drug Name

Drug Uses

Side Effects

Notes

Drug Name

Drug Uses

Side Effects

Notes

Drug Name

Drug Uses

Side Effects

Notes

Drug Name

_____

Drug Uses

Side Effects

Notes

Drug Name

Drug Uses

Side Effects

Notes

Drug Name

Drug Uses

Side Effects

Notes

Drug Name

Drug Uses

Side Effects

Notes

Drug Name

Drug Uses

Side Effects

Notes

Drug Name

Drug Uses

Side Effects

Notes

Drug Name

Drug Uses

Side Effects

Notes

Drug Name

Drug Uses

Side Effects

Notes

Drug Name

Drug Uses

Side Effects

Notes

Drug Name

Drug Uses

Side Effects

Notes

Drug Name

Drug Uses

Side Effects

Notes

Drug Name

_____

Drug Uses

```
┌─────────────────────────────────────────┐
│                                         │
│                                         │
│                                         │
│                                         │
│                                         │
└─────────────────────────────────────────┘
```

Side Effects

```
┌─────────────────────────────────────────┐
│                                         │
│                                         │
│                                         │
│                                         │
│                                         │
└─────────────────────────────────────────┘
```

Notes

Drug Name

Drug Uses

Side Effects

Notes

Drug Name

Drug Uses

Side Effects

Notes

Drug Name

Drug Uses

Side Effects

Notes

Drug Name

Drug Uses

Side Effects

Notes

Drug Name

Drug Uses

Side Effects

Notes

Drug Name

Drug Uses

Side Effects

Notes

Drug Name

Drug Uses

Side Effects

Notes

Made in the USA
Coppell, TX
16 June 2023

18160599R00111